GIANT MEAT-EATING DINOSAURS

BY **"DINO" DON LESSEM**

ILLUSTRATIONS BY **JOHN BINDON**

LERNER PUBLICATIONS COMPANY / MINNEAPOLIS

To Professor Rodolfo Coria and family: A giant among hunters of meat-eating dinosaurs

This book is available in two editions:
Library binding by Lerner Publications Company, a division of Lerner Publishing Group
Soft cover by First Avenue Editions, an imprint of Lerner Publishing Group
241 First Avenue North
Minneapolis, MN 55401 U.S.A.

Website address: www.lernerbooks.com

Library of Congress Cataloging-in-Publication-Data

Lessem, Don.
    Giant meat-eating dinosaurs / by Don Lessem ; illustrations by John Bindon.
        p.   cm. — (Meet the dinosaurs)
    Includes index.
    Summary: Describes how giant carnivorous dinosaurs hunted, as well as how scientists have learned
about them through fossil studies.
    ISBN 0-8225-3925-X (lib. bdg. : alk. paper)
    ISBN 0-8225-5326-0 (pbk. : alk. paper)
    1. Dinosaurs—Juvenile literature. 2. Carnivora, Fossil—Juvenile literature. (1. Dinosaurs. 2. Fossils.)
I. Bindon, John, ill. II. Title.
QE861.5.L477 2005
567.912—dc21

                                                                                    2002154235

Manufactured in the United States of America
1 2 3 4 5 6 – DP – 10 09 08 07 06 05

TABLE OF CONTENTS

MEET THE GIANT MEAT EATERS

WELCOME, DINOSAUR FANS!

I'm "Dino" Don. Dinosaurs are my favorite animals. Some of the scariest dinosaurs that ever lived were meat-eating giants. Here are the fast facts on the ones you'll meet in this book. Have fun!

ALBERTOSAURUS **(al-BUR-tuh-SAWR-uhs)**
Length: 26 feet
Home: western North America
Time: 70 million years ago

ALLOSAURUS **(AL-uh-SAWR-uhs)**
Length: 35 feet
Home: western North America
Time: 150 million years ago

CARCHARODONTOSAURUS
(kahr-KAYR-uh-DOHN-tuh-SAWR-uhs)
Length: 40 feet
Home: northern Africa
Time: 100 million years ago

DELTADROMEUS **(DEHL-tuh-DROH-me-uhs)**
Length: 26 feet
Home: northern Africa
Time: 97 million years ago

DILOPHOSAURUS **(dy-LOH-fuh-SAWR-uhs)**
Length: 20 feet
Home: eastern Asia, western North America
Time: 200 million years ago

GIGANOTOSAURUS
(JIHG-uh-NOH-tuh-SAWR-uhs)
Length: 45 feet
Home: southern South America
Time: 100 million years ago

SPINOSAURUS **(SPY-nuh-SAWR-uhs)**
Length: at least 40 feet
Home: northern Africa
Time: 97 million years ago

TYRANNOSAURUS REX
(tih-RAN-uh-SAWR-uhs REKS)
Length: 40 feet
Home: western North America
Time: 65 million years ago
Nickname: *T. rex*

WELCOME TO DINOSAUR TIME

Look out! *Tyrannosaurus rex* is attacking. This *Triceratops* is in trouble. Even its long horns won't save it from the giant meat eater.

T. rex has sharp teeth the size of bananas.
One bite can crush many bones of a
smaller dinosaur like *Triceratops*.

THE TIME OF THE GIANT MEAT EATERS

Dilophosaurus

Allosaurus

228 million
years ago

200 million
years ago

Dinosaurs like *T. rex* and *Triceratops* lived
millions of years ago, long before
humans. Dinosaurs were like reptiles in
some ways. They laid eggs, just as
turtles and many other reptiles do. Some
kinds of dinosaurs had scaly skin.

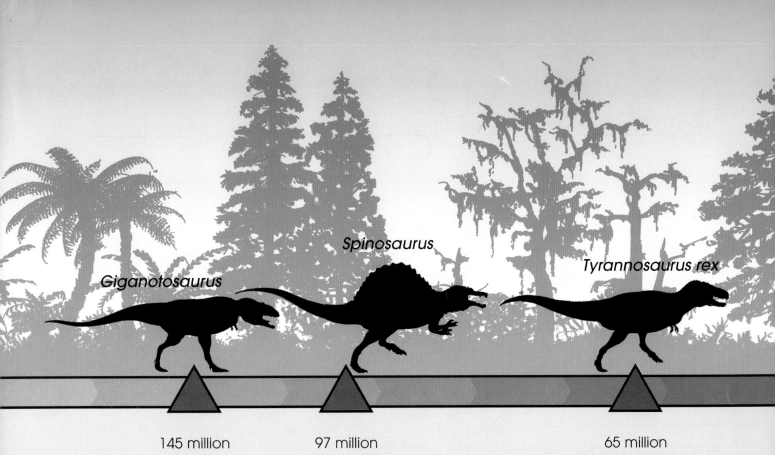

Giganotosaurus

Spinosaurus

Tyrannosaurus rex

145 million
years ago

97 million
years ago

65 million
years ago

But dinosaurs weren't reptiles. Birds are closer relatives of dinosaurs than reptiles are. Most reptiles waddle on bent legs. Most dinosaurs walked with their legs held straight under the body, like a bird does. People walk the same way.

DINOSAUR SIZES

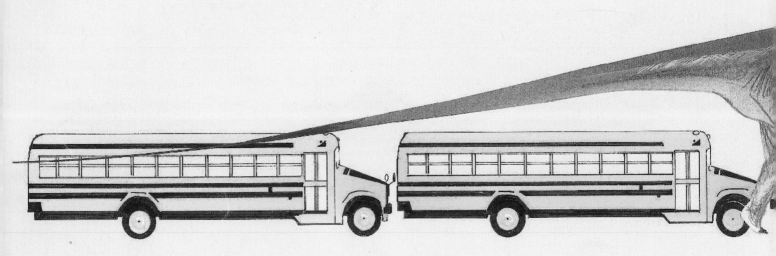

Most kinds of dinosaurs ate plants. Some kinds ate meat. Many meat eaters were **predators**, animals that hunt and eat other animals. Meat-eating dinosaurs walked on two legs. Their bones were hollow, like the bones of birds.

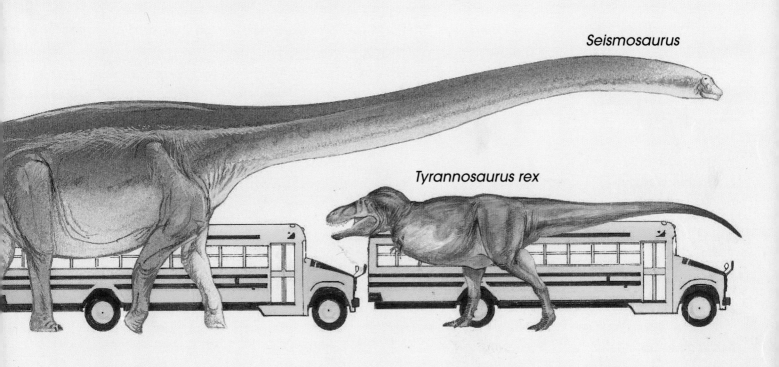

Seismosaurus

Tyrannosaurus rex

Some meat eaters were smaller than a
house cat. Others, like *Tyrannosaurus rex*,
were longer than a school bus. But the
largest plant eater, a dinosaur called
Seismosaurus, was longer than four
school buses!

DINOSAUR FOSSIL FINDS

The numbers on the map on page 13 show some of the places where people have found fossils of the dinosaurs in this book. You can match each number on the map to the name and picture of the dinosaurs on this page.

1. Albertosaurus
2. Allosaurus
3. Carcharodontosaurus
4. Deltadromeus

5. Dilophosaurus
6. Giganotosaurus
7. Spinosaurus
8. Tyrannosaurus rex

We have learned all we know about dinosaurs from their **fossils**. Fossils are traces of creatures that lived long ago. Bones, footprints, and teeth help scientists guess how dinosaurs lived. We can even find out what dinosaurs ate by studying poop fossils!

Fossils can't tell us everything about
dinosaurs. We can only guess what color a
dinosaur was and how it survived in its
dangerous world. Let's take a trip through
dinosaur time and find out what we've
learned about the giant meat eaters.

ON THE HUNT

We are in South America, 100 million years ago. A pack of *Giganotosaurus* has surrounded a huge, frightened plant eater. *Giganotosaurus* is the largest meat eater that people have discovered. It weighed 20,000 pounds, as much as two elephants!

Giganotosaurus may have hunted on its own, easily slicing smaller animals with its long, sharp teeth. And a pack of *Giganotosaurus* might have been able to take on this enormous *Argentinosaurus*.

A pair of hungry *Tyrannosaurus rex* fight in western North America, 65 million years ago. Scientists don't think that these giants hunted each other. But they may have fought over food or space.

T. rex was probably the smartest, fastest, and most powerful giant meat eater. Its sharp eyesight and sense of smell helped it track **prey**, the animals it killed and ate. Its huge jaws could rip off more than 200 pounds of meat in one bite.

It is 150 million years ago in western North America. *Allosaurus* is the king of this dinosaur world. This *Allosaurus* has just tackled a *Stegosaurus* with its three-fingered hands.

Scientists think that clawed hands and
powerful arms helped many giant meat
eaters bring down their prey. Could you
have escaped from a hungry *Allosaurus*?
Maybe! You're smarter than it was. You're
probably faster too.

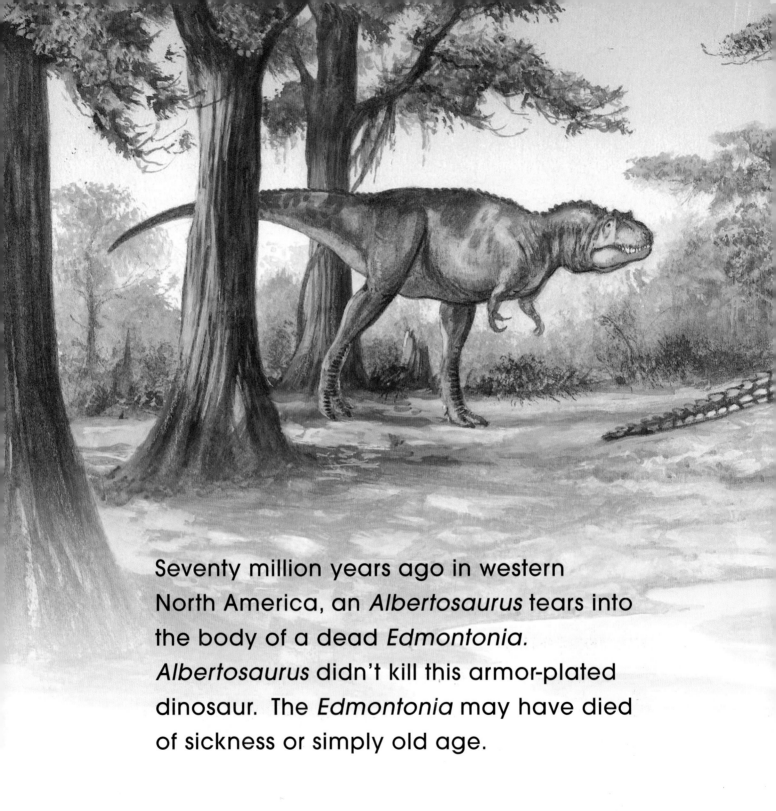

Seventy million years ago in western
North America, an *Albertosaurus* tears into
the body of a dead *Edmontonia*.
Albertosaurus didn't kill this armor-plated
dinosaur. The *Edmontonia* may have died
of sickness or simply old age.

Many giant meat eaters were probably
scavengers as well as hunters.
Scavengers find and eat the bodies of
dead animals. Vultures and coyotes are
two scavengers from our time.

LIFE AND DEATH

How did giant meat eaters grow and live?
We don't have enough information from
fossils to know for sure. But fossils have
shown us that dinosaurs hatched from
eggs. A giant meat eater's egg was
probably twice as big as a football!

Could baby giant meat eaters hunt?
Maybe. Or their parents may have brought
them strips of meat. These *Dilophosaurus*
are feeding their young in eastern Asia, 200
million years ago.

We are in a forest in northern Africa, 100 million years ago. Four young giant meat eaters are wrestling and biting each other. These *Carcharodontosaurus* aren't really fighting. They're playing.

Many predators of our time, such as lions, wolves, and house cats, learn to hunt by play-fighting. Maybe meat-eating dinosaurs did too.

Even a giant meat eater could be eaten.
We are in northern Africa, 97 million years
ago. Here a pack of *Deltadromeus* feeds
on the body of a *Spinosaurus*. This sail-
backed giant may have died of sickness or
old age. Or maybe the speedy
Deltadromeus killed it.

A dead giant meat eater would have made a great feast for scavengers. *Spinosaurus* may have grown as long as 60 feet—the size of three *Dilophosaurus*! Scientists haven't found enough fossils to be sure.

Our journey through dinosaur time ends 65 million years ago. Many scientists think that's when an object from space called an **asteroid** smashed into Earth. The asteroid may have changed Earth's weather by causing fires and making volcanoes erupt.

Those weather changes may be the
reason that the last dinosaurs died out.
They were wiped out long before people
lived on Earth. But the birds we know
today are close cousins of some meat-
eating dinosaurs. Some scientists think that
birds really are dinosaurs!

The giant meat eaters are gone. But they left behind many clues about their lives. Scientists found this *Giganotosaurus* skull and many other bones. The skull is much bigger than the human skull that sits in its mouth in this picture.

The bones were dug out of a hillside and
sent to a museum for cleaning. Then they
were copied. A skeleton was built with the
copied bones. *Giganotosaurus* stands long
and tall once again. This giant meat eater
is one scary dinosaur even without its skin!

GLOSSARY

asteroid (AS-tur-oyd): a large, rocky lump that moves in space

fossils (FAH-suhlz): the bones, tracks, or traces of something that lived long ago

predators (PREH-duh-turz): animals that hunt and eat other animals

prey (PRAY): an animal that other animals hunt and eat

scavengers (SKA-vehn-jurz): animals that eat the bodies of dead animals

INDEX